A Sa
Way

David O'Malley SDB

When Don Bosco sent his first
missionaries to South America, he
was photographed handing Fr John
Cagliero, who headed the expedition,
the book of the Rule as if to say:

*I would like to go with you myself,
but since I cannot do so this Rule
will take my place. Keep this as you
would a precious treasure.*

Front Cover Graphic
Medal based on
The Good Shepherd in the Catacombs of Priscilla in Rome.

Back Cover Graphic
Salesian Crest 1884
Motto
DA MIHI ANIMAS CAETERA TOLLE
GIVE ME SOULS TAKE AWAY THE REST

Published by
Don Bosco Publications
Thornleigh House
Sharples Park
BOLTON BL1 6PQ
www.don-bosco-publications.co.uk
sarah@salesians.org.uk
© 2014
ISBN 978-1-909080-11-9

Fonts used
Main Text Calibri
Headings **Book Antiqua Bold**
Introduction Bookman Old Style 11pt

Printed by
Buxton Press Limited
Palace Road, Buxton, Derbyshire, SK17 6AE

Foreword

This text is offered to all who find themselves at home with Salesian spirituality, whatever their Church or faith background. While in some ways it is similar to the rule of life to which many vowed Salesians commit themselves, the Salesian Way of Life will find a home with so many more people. Whether single or married, in family life or at work, alone or with others, this way of life provokes deeper spiritual reflection on experience. St Francis de Sales, the patron of all Salesian spirituality, believed that the awareness of the mystery of God could be a continuous source of strength and meaning in all the events of a person's life. Such awareness leads to greater resilience and balance in life. Those of us who struggle with the busyness of life will find in Salesian spirituality an inner strength awakened through the ordinary events of life.

This way of Don Bosco is therefore an invitation to explore your own spiritual depths, not in the reflections of deep theology but in the daily routines and thought patterns of each day. It is offered to you as part of our celebrations for the 200th anniversary of the birth of Don Bosco. He made this spirituality available to those who worked with the young but it applies to all relationships and to individuals. The spirituality you find described here is outgoing, optimistic, gentle and ordinary. May it strengthen your resilience and increase your commitment to build a better world.

Fr Martin Coyle SDB
Provincial of the Salesian GBR Province

Contents

To the weak I became weak,
that I might win the weak.
I have become all things to all people,
that by all means I might save some.
I do it all for the sake of the gospel,
that I may share with them in its blessings.

1 Corinthians 9:22-23 (NRSV)

Introduction

Statue of Margaret Bosco

Pathways

The Gospel way traced out in Salesian spirituality can be seen to be an amalgamation of three different pathways:

* The path of St Francis de Sales, a Doctor of the Church in the 16th Century.

* The way of raising children, used by St John Bosco's own mother Margaret.

* The way of working that St John Bosco developed through his work with the youth of Turin in the 19th century.

These three paths merge into a way of life that can guide many busy people in their work, in family life, in raising children, in personal growth in holiness and in building community. The Salesian pathway is a way into living the Gospel and a way of building the Church, especially for the young.

The Salesian tradition is therefore one of the major pathways of heart-centred lay spirituality in the Church. As the Church becomes more lay-focussed and less clerical, Salesian spirituality has much to offer in responding to the challenge of secular culture.

This way of life attempts to capture the Salesian spirituality of the ordinary. It is not meant to be clever and it requires little prior knowledge to appreciate. The energy of Salesian spirituality comes from mindfulness of a loving Father within each person. This awareness gives hope, deepens meaning and lends resilience to relationships. This way of life is intended to strengthen the awareness of a loving Father so that, as Don Bosco reminded us, *People should not only be loved but they should know that they are loved.*

A Dedication to Margaret Bosco

This way of life is dedicated to Don Bosco's mother, Margaret. Her experience of raising a family on her own formed the setting within which Don Bosco discovered his vocation. Her belief in the goodness of all her children was the crucible within which Don Bosco later recognised a unique way to join ordinary life and the presence of God. Despite the regular battles between her three boys, Margaret was able to manage the tensions and also keep her own sense of inner peace.

Much of what Don Bosco wrote as an adult is rooted in that family experience. Through Margaret's family leadership he found cheerfulness, optimism, discipline and reflection combined into a maternal approach that created a family spirit. Don Bosco was able to take that experience and make it available to teachers, care workers, youth workers and parents. Margaret was not able to write anything but in many ways she is the author of Don Bosco's spirituality. Even two hundred years later, she would recognise much of what is written here.

Francis de Sales – His Spirituality

St Francis de Sales, with St Jane de Chantal, established a Salesian school of spirituality during the tensions of the Post-Reformation. His approach to sectarian tension was to engage with friendship. So whilst Protestants and Catholics were besieging each other's towns, Francis was asking people to use the battering rams of loving kindness to break through to the hearts of others. Francis said that it is easier to catch bees with a spoonful of honey than with a barrel full of vinegar.

Francis worked to reassure lay people that they can be holy in the kitchen as well as in the cloister. He rooted holiness in an awareness of a loving Father who always has us by the hand whatever happens. He wrote for lay people, helping them to live mindful of that interior devout life that is the mystical core of each person. Margaret Bosco never read a book but she lived intuitively the spirituality of St Francis de Sales. Together with Don Bosco, she opened up the spirituality of St Francis de Sales for parents, youth workers and teachers. Readers of all faiths, married or single, will find in this way of life a practical entry point into the wisdom of St Francis de Sales.

11

Father and Teacher of Youth

John Bosco was raised in poverty in Northern Italy at a time of war and famine. His father died when he was only two years old. In his family life, despite huge tensions and insecurity, John discovered an interior life that built on the faith of his mother. His call to priesthood led him eventually to Turin where he discovered the streets full of abandoned young people. All his instincts, inspired by his family experience, led him to respond to these young people's needs with the wisdom of his own mother.

As a priest, Don Bosco developed a way of working that created a home, a school, a church and a playground for young people. He did all this not in an institutional way but with a family Spirit. He wanted to build relationships through respect, understanding, affection and humour. His approach was built on the friendly presence of mature adults who were skilled at living mindfully in the presence of a loving Father. That awareness is what still gives adults who live Salesian spirituality the resilience, cheerfulness and patience to build healthy relationships.

A Way of Life

This small book uses the word *Way* in its title. In some respects it resembles the first part of the rule of life followed by vowed Salesians. It is not a list of rules but rather a way of living. All religious orders in the Catholic Church have a rule or a constitution which directs the way that they live. This short pathway is therefore an attempt to connect ordinary life with a deeper spirituality. Many of the lay people within the wider Salesian network have expressed the need for a way to reflect on their own way of living Salesian spirituality as a student, as a parent or grandparent.

For many in the Salesian network who work with youth, it has been clear for many years how the preventive system integrates their work with the young into a deeper awareness of life. This rule of life is an invitation to explore how Salesian spirituality can inform all of life: relationships, illness, marriage, bereavement and so on. It is a small contribution to the renewal of Salesian spirituality as we celebrate Don Bosco's Bicentenary.

Our Way of Life

Don Bosco – Turin 1861

1. Presence

As a Salesian you are called to recognise
the presence of a wisdom and an inner teacher
who has been with you
since the beginning of your journey.
You are invited to embrace this presence,
as it embraces you, with gratitude and humility.
Despite all the uncertainties and losses
that life brings, this presence remains.
It abides as a growing relationship
that eventually makes sense of all your experience.
For better or for worse you are held and cherished
in this eternal and intimate presence.
Learning to trust this presence in yourself
and awaken it in others is part of your Salesian vocation.
Exploring the lessons of loving kindness
scattered through each day
is part of the mystical pathway into meaning
for every Salesian, whether vowed or lay.
On that pathway you will meet both the cross
and the resurrection, sometimes on the same day
and even in the same events.
The sense of being in the presence of this mystery
brings a depth and significance to the smallest events.
Like a good friend,
this presence draws back the surface veil of your life
to reveal the deeper energy of a Gospel wisdom
and a love that moves all creation.

2. Moved by an Inner Spirit

Sensitive to the promptings of this Spiritual presence,
you are called to become a sign and bearer
of love for all people
but especially the young and the abandoned.
This calling comes from your giftedness
which gives you the skills to care for others,
but it also comes from your brokenness
which gives you the compassion to care for others.
You may be driven by the call for justice
through this inner Spirit to make huge sacrifices
for young people at risk.
You may be called by compassion
to live a healing gentleness
among young people, family and friends.
Let the Spirit of justice and compassion
move you so that your life becomes
a sign and bearer of love for others.
Study St Francis de Sales and Don Bosco
so that their wisdom focusses the Spirit
at work in you and brings it into action.

3. A Worldwide Network

The Spirit that moves you to work in a Salesian way
has moved many others in the past and present
in all parts of the world.
The personal call to live Salesian spirituality
is part of a worldwide family Spirit.
You will find a family likeness in many others
who have been called like you to be signs and bearers
of loving kindness especially for the young.
The Spirit moves you
and breaks down misunderstandings,
building bridges between nationalities.
The Salesian preventive system
becomes a common culture
that allows people of different traditions
to live together.
The Salesian vision builds a global village
and a human family
that transcends the differences of race and creed.
Be confident in this global vision
and allow it to strengthen your ability
to live in a multicultural world.

4. Awakening a Family Likeness

You need not be afraid
to speak about the Spirit
that draws and sometimes drives you into action
for others,
because the same Spirit
lives in every other person you will meet.
In wordless ways your engagement with others
will awaken the same Spirit in the lives of others.
The scriptures remind us that everyone
moved by this Spirit
is a son or a daughter of God.
So it is as if you are recognising a family likeness
in yourself and others,
a likeness that makes each person a sacrament:
an outward sign of God's inner presence.
Therefore every gathering
of two or three people
is potentially a family reunion
when viewed through the eyes of love,
of justice
and of compassion.
Every young person you meet,
however damaged or intolerant,
is always a son or a daughter of God.
Ask for the gift of eyes to see that reality
in all your relationships.

5. The Call to Belong

You will not be able to do this work
of recognising the presence of God on your own.
You cannot be Salesian on your own.
Everyone you meet is both your pupil and your teacher
whatever their age or status.
Your Salesian call is a call into a wider community
and into a network of care for others.
Yours is a vocation to interdependence;
to giving and receiving
in a way that challenges
the individualism of many cultures.
You too can lose touch
with the still small voice of the Spirit
unless you are aware of your need of others.
There are no solo Salesians,
no macho heroes,
just people who share their fortunes
and fragility
in a teamwork
that can transform lives.
This mutual enrichment creates a sacred space
where all people, especially the young,
can grow at their own pace into the fullness of life.

6. Family Roots of Our Vocation

The Salesian way of life emerged
through a combination of the wisdom
of St Francis de Sales and the experience of Don Bosco
with his mother Margaret in their family life.
Here Don Bosco learnt about loving kindness, hard work
and an awareness of God's mysterious presence
in ordinary events.
Later he recognised in his mother's life
the deep wisdom of St Francis de Sales,
especially his gentleness,
his balance and an optimism
rooted in the presence of a loving Father.
The loss of his own Father at an early age
led Don Bosco to a compassion and energy
for all those abandoned youth that he found in Turin.
In a similar way you have been called
through your experience
to encounter the mystery of God
and have discovered a vocation
to serve those who are abandoned
or on the edge of life.
Your early years will already be rich
with the roots of your own Salesian vocation.
Return often to the story of the Spirit
at work in both the light and dark
of your own youth and childhood.

7. The Salesian Model

Your Salesian vocation
is also shaped by the experience of Don Bosco
working with inner city youth.
Don Bosco developed his family-based spirituality
into a way of life
during his time working with youth in Turin.
There he created a home, a school, a church
and a playground for abandoned youth.
These four areas form a balanced way of living
for the whole of your life.
Don Bosco began with a playground,
a place where people could relax and renew themselves.
Then he created a school
where people could grow and change.
Later he built a home where the abandoned could belong
and finally he built a church
where the presence of God could become more visible.
Belonging, learning, relaxing and meaning
are Salesian ways of making sense of your life
and also rebalancing your life when things go wrong.
Year by year you will learn
to turn these values outwards to others in service.
Year by year you will also learn to look inwards
and let these same values balance your inner life.
It is the same Spiritual pathway that reaches inwards
into your heart and also carries you outwards
to build a better world alongside the young.

8. A Gospel Pathway

Your sense of being Salesian
is charged with the wisdom of the Gospel;
the wisdom of the Good Shepherd,
the Good Samaritan,
the Beatitudes and the Easter mystery.
The path to which you are drawn
by the Spirit is a Gospel pathway
that leads to cross and to resurrection.
It is a path of renunciation, of service, of joy
and also of trust in confusion.
It is a path of determination
to protect the Spirit of the young,
a path of obstinacy in preventing harm
and of cheerful resistance to becoming hard-hearted.
This Gospel pathway,
traced out in Salesian spirituality,
reveals the work of parents and teachers as a vocation,
a journey of self-emptying
rather than simply being a phase or a career in life.
The Salesian calling lays bare the drama of your life
as it is poured out in love and hope
for a future that is not your own.

9. Mary

The mother of Jesus stands
as a beacon on your journey
because she was able to face confusion
and keep on trusting.
From the moment the angel appeared to her
when she was a young girl,
her life was marked by turmoil and questions until,
at the foot of the cross,
she embraced her son after his brutal death.
And yet her trust, despite this confusion,
led her to allow Christ to grow within her
and helped her to give Christ to the world.
You too are challenged
to recognise the presence that you carry
and awaken it in the world around you.
Like Mary, you will meet confusion and failure
and like her, you will persevere in trusting the road
that you have taken.
Therefore every Salesian project and plan
is dedicated to this woman
who trusted the Spirit to move in her
and allowed her life to be turned upside down.
It is her silent presence
that marked the growth of the Gospel,
and that presence will continue
to bless and guide you on your Salesian journey
through all generations.

23

10. Loving Kindness

The only proper responses to this presence
living within you and in those around you
are gratitude and loving kindness.
Gratitude opens you up to receive a family Spirit
moving in all people and in creation.
Loving kindness becomes the outward sign
of the respect for this sacred presence
living at the heart of all people.
Loving kindness builds bridges between people;
it breaks through the isolation of individuals
and builds community.
Loving kindness heals the hurts
that give rise to anger and injustice.
Loving kindness will test your faith
and self-discipline in dealing with others.
The Gospel also invites you
to love your neighbour as yourself,
and so it is also important that loving kindness
is turned inwards into a balanced gentleness
with yourself.
You cannot give what you have not got
and so your own life needs to be rooted
in a loving kindness to yourself
as well as to other people.

11. Love Shown in Action

Loving kindness is a common value
at the root of most major religious traditions.
The Salesian tradition opens up a Gospel pattern
of loving kindness
that becomes a practical way of living.
It is the energy that drives you outwards
to make the first move for others.
It also invites you inwards
to touch the Spirit that moves your soul.
Through loving kindness
you are also caught up into the love
that moves all creation.
Do not let this loving kindness
descend into a soft sentimentality.
The one who loves
will not shy away from setting reasonable demands;
as a competent surgeon
will not hesitate to cause pain in order to heal.
Likewise you too should not hold back
from inspiring, cajoling, challenging
and persevering in the task of serving souls.
Let your actions speak of loving kindness,
of justice and of compassion.
In this way the energy of the Spirit
and the needs of the world are linked
and you become a source of good news for others.

12. Compassion

Compassion opens your eyes
to the need for loving kindness in the lives of others.
Pain, sadness and violence
reveal an emptiness in life
that will often find an echo in your own life.
The emptiness of young people's lives in Don Bosco's Turin
resonated with the troubles of his own childhood.
So too, the difficulties and absences in others' lives
can reveal your own call,
through frailty and through your gifts,
to a loving kindness marked by compassion.
In this way you will learn to recognise
the call of God in and through the lessons of life
and especially through honest friendships.
Do not be afraid to express your compassion
for those who struggle,
nor be afraid to express your disappointment
with those who have let you down.
Especially, do not hide your own need for compassion
since it is not good to be alone
when you are under pressure.
Your spirituality is heart-centred.
So, when you can,
speak your deepest truth
to those who can support you on the journey.

13. Relationships – Sacred Spaces

Loving kindness reveals itself in Salesian living
as a desire to draw others
into a network of belonging
that leads to mutual growth.
Your relationships, with differing levels of intensity,
are a school for the soul.
It is here that difficulties are shared,
hearts are opened
and hurts are healed.
It is also the place where life is shared and celebrated
and its meaning explored in a belonging
that breaks through to eternity.
Such love lasts forever
so that your family, work-place and friendships
become sacred places
where tenderness, truth and respect
combine to bring people to fullness of life.
Try to create spaces
where each person is free
and rules are clear and kept to a minimum.
In leadership learn to serve,
to listen and to stand your ground.
Speak your truth in kindness and sincerity.
Do not stand aloof or run away from belonging.
It is the only place where you can become real.

14. Shepherding Hope

As a Salesian you are called to focus
on the good you find and help it to grow
rather than moan from the touchline of life.
St Paul reminds us to fill our minds
with all that is right, good, pure and true
in order to stay at peace with God.
Seeing goodness and celebrating it in people,
despite their other faults,
will build up your sense of community
and strengthen your resilience.
Distracting people away from gossip and grumbling
will set them free to count their blessings
and choose to hope.
Don Bosco said
that the better was always the enemy of the good.
Remember that hope is always locked
into the present moment, imperfect as it is,
because that is the only place
where you meet the mystery of God.
Therefore nurture hope in yourself,
trust your own goodness and through that trust,
shepherd hope in the lives of others.
Take care to focus on what is positive
and help it to grow
rather than pick on faults and highlight them.
In this way you will be imitating the life of Jesus
who did not break the crushed reed
or put out the smouldering flame.

15. Self-Sacrifice

Don Bosco said to the young people of Turin,
For you I study, for you I work, for you I live,
for you I am ready even to give my life.
Your ability to go the extra mile
in the care and safeguarding of others
will witness to the sacredness of all human life.
Such generosity opens up the fortress of people's hearts
and sets them free to believe and trust again.
Parents, teachers and friends pour out their lives
on a daily basis for the good of others
often with no recognition.
You are called to support such loving kindness.
Not one of these generous acts is lost
because they are all an expression
of a deep fatherly motherly love that moves all creation.
Your ability to escape from self-centred thinking
and move to self-sacrifice
is the journey that gives your life meaning and direction.
It is the gift of oneself, poured out in service
especially for the young and abandoned,
which marks the Salesian path to fullness of life.
Parents, grandparents, teachers and youth workers
walk this path every day
and, whether they know it or not,
they walk in the presence of God.
As a Salesian you are called to support those
who journey with the needy and awaken in them
the mystical dimension of their care for others.

16. Little Ones

Whatever your gender
there is something maternal
about the way that you are called
to respond to frailty in others or in yourself.
There should be no room for harshness in your life
but rather a gentle and consistent discipline
that ensures freedom and space to grow strong
where life is broken.
This is not a sentimental or smothering attachment
but a deep desire to see broken people
come to life and grow into mature independence.
Challenge those damaged by life
to maintain gentleness with themselves
whilst also encouraging them
to explore their unique pathway with courage.
Make the first move
in responding to the needs of the vulnerable
you find in your world.
Look beneath the brash bravado
or the shrinking shyness of others to see the face of God.
Create opportunities for conversation,
engage in the world of the poor and abandoned
and allow them to test the strength of your care.
Let their needs clarify your call into the future.
Your capacity for loving kindness
will be stretched beyond comfort
so that you will be led to share
something of the cross on your road to resurrection.

17. Talking to God on the Road

Your visible life might be busy or quiet
but your hidden inner life will always be sustained
by a heart-to-heart conversation with God.
This conversation can arise from an inner dialogue
with the Spirit that inspires and guides.
Sometimes that Spirit will move
your emotions or your mind
to new insights or to take action.
Often you will be invited simply
to be at play in this presence.
At other times events will provoke your reflection
and become inspiration.
Your reflection on the road begins
by allowing your life experience to speak and lead,
through contemplation, back to life.
Therefore your prayer should be rooted in reality,
reflected upon with the faith that you have.
Salesian prayer is not a private activity
but involves an awareness of the complexity
of relationships that sustain life and community.
Your prayerful reflection is not separate from activity.
Salesian prayer bubbles up in the middle of busyness
in the way that lovers come to each other's minds
when apart.
Salesian prayer is continuous but not always conscious.

18. Hospitality

Every Salesian home, parish, school or project
is a place of hospitality and welcome.
The quality of your sustained welcome
makes every encounter a sacred space
where people can feel safe, relax
and be present just as they are.
*Whenever you welcome one of these little ones,
you welcome me,* said Jesus.
So hospitality for you must also become an act of faith
in the unique Spirit at the heart of each individual.
Hospitality is hard on the gift of time;
it requires adaptation and flexibility,
self-sacrifice and patience.
Your hospitality may need structure and timetables
so that others feel secure,
It may need flexibility and a good listening ear.
In both situations you are called to look, listen
and sense how you are being invited
to respond by the Spirit that moves you.
The encounter between Mary and Elizabeth
at the Visitation gives you a model for hospitality.
Mary made the first move to reach out to her cousin
and in that generous act the presence of God within her
was awakened and recognised.
In the same way you are called to make the first move in
welcoming others but also ready to recognise
the movement of the Spirit within you.

19. Resurrection

As a Salesian you are called to interpret all events
in the light of resurrection.
The Resurrection was a silent event
that came as a complete surprise to its first witnesses.
Therefore be ever on the lookout for hidden resurrections.
They may appear in deeper changes of heart
in family or friends, in opportunities opening up,
in generosity, compassion and coincidences.
Live in the hope of resurrection now
through a trust that new life
will eventually emerge from struggle and loss.
Learn to put struggle and loss
into the wider pattern of cross and resurrection,
and draw from that pattern the resilience
to persevere through to the surprise of Easter.
Whilst the hard realities of an unjust world
and the need to struggle for change may fill your days,
it is also true that the horizon of your life
is always focussed on Easter.
Resurrection is therefore a process
that accompanies you throughout life
so that each act of reconciliation, each new discovery
and every genuine smile that you meet
easters in[1] you towards new life.

1. Let him easter in us, be a dayspring to the dimness of us, be a crimson-cresseted east. (Gerard Manley Hopkins, *The Wreck of the Deutschland*.)

20. The Eucharist

For you the Eucharist is the liturgy of all your life.
Every meal shared, every word spoken
and every group gathered
has the potential to reveal the presence of God.
As you listen to the word in church,
as you break bread with others,
remember that this sacrament is the outward sign
of a reality that fills all of your life.
When you break through to a young person
in caring conversation,
the presence of God is again broken open and shared.
As you pour out your life in selfless service
you share the Eucharistic sacrifice of Jesus.
Your service becomes
a kind of sacrament of God's presence for others.
Seeing life through the eyes of Jesus in the Gospels
brings significance and meaning to the simplest experiences.
As you eat and drink at Communion,
the bread and wine become part of you
and you become bread and wine for others.
Therefore the Eucharist reveals the intimate union
between your life and the risen Jesus.
The intimacy of this risen presence moving in your life
goes beyond your understanding.
Just try to live this mystery of intimacy
with the risen Lord and allow it to shape your life
and deepen your friendship with Jesus.

21. Young People

Young people
are the burning bush of your Salesian life.
They reveal the presence of God,
clarify your call and illuminate the path to the future.
As you engage with the young,
you will recognise in their passion the power
to heal hurts and to renew the face of the earth.
Youth is also the holy ground
where generations meet together
and explore new reasons for living and hoping.
Don Bosco described this relationship
between the young and adults
as a kind of electric current
that flows between people.
Sometimes there will be sparks
but let the family Spirit
focus this energy and use it to build a better world.
Young people
may also include your own children and grandchildren
as well as those more formal relationships
in education and youth ministry.

22. The Needs of the Young

Remember that young people
are also the most vulnerable part of society,
your special concern as a Salesian.
Some of their needs will speak to your heart
and call you to action
but realise
that you cannot meet all the needs you recognise.
Take your concerns for the young
into your reflection
and allow the Spirit to speak to your heart.
Discern before you act,
seeking out a wise guide when you are confused.
Then, make your stand with the needs of the young
that you can meet
and leave the rest of those needs in God's hands.

23. A Youthful Spirituality

As you grow older on your Salesian journey
maintain a youthful spirituality.
That spirituality
is marked by all the best aspects of youth:
optimism, energy for change, generosity,
passion for life, idealism, joy and flexibility.
Meeting life with these values
allows you to stay close to youth
and draw their energy into building honest citizens
and good Christians for the future.
This youthful spirituality
leads you to support and empower young people
so that they grow in ownership of their world.
Step by step you are called to relinquish control
so that young people increase in leadership
as you step back into the shadows.
Stepping back and letting go is part of your cross
that is hidden beneath
the cheerful optimism of Salesian spirituality.
Another aspect of the cross
is the constant need to begin again
in engaging with new situations and young people
as they grow older and move on.
You are challenged in your work with the young
not to cling but instead to bless young people
with the freedom to move away
on their own journey through life.

24. Conflict

There is no real growth without confusion.
You will meet misunderstandings
in friendships and at work.
You will learn to unlock the learning
such conflicts contain
when you live Don Bosco's preventive system.
Treat others with respect and withdraw when anger
might lead you to damage the Spirit of another person.
Try to understand their situation and their blind spots
and do not assume motives but stay with facts.
Show warmth and kindness
when confronted with anger and frustration
even if you are annoyed.
Use a quiet word in the ear to resolve tensions
rather than humiliate others in public
or gossip about them.
Try to be optimistic and cheerful
about maintaining a relationship into the future.
Underneath all these approaches
call to mind that each person involved in a dispute
is a son or daughter of God.
It is your role to be reasonable,
to guard the souls of those involved
and take time to reflect on the conflict.
In this way the conflict becomes a lesson
and the cross of conflict is once more transformed
into new life for all those involved.

25. Friendship

As a Salesian
you are called to be a friend especially to the young.
Don Bosco is known as the friend of youth
and lived with a warmth and energy
which you too must carry to the world.
A friend is one who sets other people free
to be themselves,
so ensure that your friendship liberates
rather than confines others.
Friendship is part of the mystery
of the communion of saints, establishing ties of love
that even death will not break.
So your friendships take you into the mystery
of who you are and who you will become.
Looked at with spiritual eyes
your friendships are already
an expression of a mystical union with life.
Your friendships are rooted in an eternal meaning.
Therefore treasure friendships
as the place where heart speaks to heart,
where weaknesses are revealed and hurts are healed.
Do not multiply many friendships
or ignore the need for communication.
Instead,
live them with an open and balanced faithfulness
so that they might bear fruit throughout your life
and in your care for the young.

26. Work

Your work is contemplation in action.
It takes you into the world of shared tasks
and builds your relationships.
Work shared with others becomes a focus
of community and of creativity.
Whatever work you do,
it is capable of transforming the world
and building the Kingdom.
The value of your work is not limited by targets or profit
but by the quality of the community
that it builds and the good that your labour achieves.
Don Bosco always linked work with temperance
so your work should be embraced
as one part of life
lived through belonging, learning, play
and the search for meaning.
Your work should therefore build community.
It should create opportunities to celebrate,
to learn and to search for meaning.
You will achieve this both in the work that is done
or in the way that the work is done.

27. Sickness and Dying

Don Bosco said that when you die
after a lifetime of living Salesian Spirituality
then a great victory has been gained
for the Salesian family.
The call to suffer illness
is an invitation to deepen the intimacy
that you feel with the Father.
It is a time of dependence on those around
and a time to recognise your own frailty.
At such times the gentleness of Salesian Spirituality
must be focussed on oneself.
St Francis de Sales encouraged those he was guiding
to pray for the gift of acceptance;
not just of the particular infirmity they had to carry
but also the timing of that infirmity
and the place and people that surrounded it.
As Salesians, we make a gift of our lives in love to God
for the service of others.
Illness and dying are aspects of that self-giving
that opens the door to heaven and Don Bosco's garden.

Daily Prayer to Saint John Bosco

Saint John Bosco,
Father and Teacher of youth,
docile to the gifts of the Spirit
and open to the reality of your times
you were for the young,
especially the little ones and the poor,
a sign of the love and the special care of God.

Be our guide
as we walk the path of friendship with the Lord Jesus,
so that we may discover in Him and in his Gospel
the meaning of our lives and the source of true happiness.
Help us to respond with generosity to the vocation we have
received from God, so that in daily life we may be builders
of communion,
and may collaborate with enthusiasm
and in communion with the whole Church
in creating a civilisation of love.

Obtain for us the grace of perseverance
in living a high standard of Christian life,
according to the Spirit of the Beatitudes;
and grant that, guided by Mary Help of Christians,
we may one day be with you
in the great family of heaven. Amen.

Salesian Crest 1884
Motto
DA MIHI ANIMAS CAETERA TOLLE
GIVE ME SOULS TAKE AWAY THE REST

Vostro aff° (affezionatissimo) amico in J. C. (Gesù Cristo)
(Your most affectionate friend in Jesus)
Sac. (Sacerdote) Gio (Giovanni) Bosco
(Firma della lettera di Roma, 10 Maggio 1884)
(Fr John Bosco)
(Signature on letter from Rome 10th May 1884)

Web Addresses

There are Salesian Web Sites all over the world

Salesians in Rome
> www.sdb.org

Salesian News Agency
> www.infoans.org

Salesian Sisters in Rome
> www.cgfmanet.org

Salesian Cooperators in the UK
> www.salesiancooperators.org.uk

Salesian Past Pupils
> www.donbosco.co.uk/pp

Salesians Ireland
> www.salesiansireland.ie

Don Bosco Youth Net
> www.donboscoyouth.net

Don Bosco's Way
> https://sites.google.com/site/dbway2010

Salesian Missions Online
> www.salesianmissions.org

Don Bosco West
> www.donboscowest.org

Youth Outreach
> www.yo.org.hk/index/?q=efirst

Catholic Youth Work
> www.catholicyouthwork.com

Vides UK
> www.videsuk.org.uk

A Good Book

A good book can enter homes
where no priest may ever go.
Those in doubt will take it as a gift, or possibly a souvenir.
There's no embarrassment in giving it,
no obligation for anyone to read.
When it's read, it calmly teaches truth.
If ignored, there's no harm done,
except possibly a lingering regret,
which may, one day, spark a desire to know the truth
which the book is always there to teach.
At times, the book may gather dust, lying on a table,
or in a bookcase, for the moment just forgotten.
Come a time, however, of loneliness, of sadness,
of just sheer boredom, of anxiety about the future,
of need for some escape,
then this half-forgotten book casts off its dust,
becomes a faithful friend, opens up some new horizons,
perhaps, as in St Augustine's case,
may even lead to conversion.
A good book is polite with those afraid of it,
for it speaks to them, without a hint of any suspicion.
With other people, it becomes a friend indeed,
ready to talk things over, to accompany them,
anywhere, at any time.
In a family, the recipient may never read it,
but a son or daughter, or perhaps a friend,
or a neighbour, might welcome it.
In a village, it may pass from hand to hand,
befriend a hundred villagers or more.
In a city, God alone knows the good a book does.
Borrowed from a library, bought in a bookshop,
found at the side of a hospital bed,
a book becomes a welcome friend.

Don Bosco

DON BOSCO PUBLICATIONS
www.don-bosco-publications.co.uk

Books by Kathleen Pearce
KATIE COMES TO MASS
ROSIE GOES TO CHURCH BOOK and DVD
CHLOE AND JACK VISIT THE VATICAN
GOOD NEWS IN THE FAMILY
OUR COLOURFUL CHURCH YEAR
101 SAINTS & SPECIAL PEOPLE
Books by Michael T Winstanley SDB
SYMBOLS and SPIRITUALITY
LENTEN SUNDAYS
DON BOSCO'S GOSPEL WAY
JESUS AND THE LITTLE PEOPLE
Books by Other Authors
SERVING THE YOUNG by James Gallagher SDB
STARTING AGAIN FROM DON BOSCO by Ian Murdoch SDB
SEAN DEVEREUX by Michael Delmer SDB
GOD OF MANY FACES by Sister Margaret Renshaw FMA
MAMMA MARGARET by Teresio Bosco SDB
BLESSED IS SHE WHO BELIEVED by J J Bartolomé SDB
TEACHER, TEACH US TO PRAY by Sister Winifred Acred FMA
THE WITNESSES by Sister Winifred Acred FMA
MOVING ON by Margaret J Cooke
DON BOSCO - THE PRIEST, THE MAN, THE TIMES by W R Ainsworth SDB
DON'T ORGANISE MY TEARS by Tony Bailey SDB
BOSCO Z BOOK Illustrated Life of Don Bosco for Children

A Salesian Way of Life

is available,

as an EBook,

on Amazon Kindle.